MAXIE THOMAS
and the
FOOT SOLDIERS

MARLISA WIGGINS

Maxie Thomas and the Foot Soldiers

Illustrator: Prabir - India

Printed in the United States of America
Keen Vision Publishing, LLC
www.publishwithkvp.com
ISBN: 979-8-9951383-0-3

To my parents, William and Delois.
Thank you for remembering those front porch visits and dinner conversations you have poured into me, making this story survive.

On December 1, 1955, Rosa Parks refused to give up her seat on a segregated bus in Montgomery, AL. With that event, civil disobedience spread across the South, leading to other Black people being willfully defiant. This act of resistance in Montgomery set the stage for similar challenges to segregation in other Alabama cities, including Tuscaloosa.

In May of 1962, three Stillman College students and a high school student were arrested for refusing to give up their seats to white passengers on a bus in downtown Tuscaloosa, Alabama. The bus stopped in front of the S. H. Kress & Co. store, and the arrests made many people in the Black community feel even more frustrated and ready for change. These protests showed how unfair life could be for Black people in Tuscaloosa, not just on buses but also in the kinds of jobs they were allowed to have.

S.H. KRESS & CO.

Oak City
Barber & Beauty
Shop
Williams Cleaners
Oak city
Barber & Beauty Shop
Murphy
Undertaking
Blue Front Co

Some Black citizens owned successful businesses, such as grocery stores, laundromats, restaurants, funeral homes, medical offices, barber shops, hair salons, and taxi services—all of which could be seen at the Blue Front District. But most Black citizens were only given the chance to work as maids, janitors, or in other low-paying jobs.

While Black citizens sought progress within their communities, resistance from state leadership reinforced the barriers of segregation. On June 11, 1963, the governor of Alabama, George Wallace, blocked the entrance to Foster Auditorium on the University of Alabama's campus to try to prevent the enrollment of two Black students, Vivian Malone and James Hood, to uphold segregation. Governor Wallace declared that Alabama would be segregated today, segregated tomorrow, and segregated forever.

DRUID
DRAGONS
Colored
Entrance

The Black citizens were agitated with the separate but not-so-equal rights. Black children attended schools and used second-hand books. Black citizens also had to enter through the backdoor areas of businesses as if they were unfit, and they could not roam freely in the city without restraints.

These daily reminders of inequality reached into nearly every part of life, including where Black families could spend their free time. Black people were only allowed to go to the Diamond Theatre to enjoy a movie. Snow Hinton, former mayor of Tuscaloosa (1969-1972), was associated with this theatre that provided Black people with entertainment they couldn't get elsewhere. When the Capri theatre was built, Black people could attend but could only watch from the balcony. They could not attend the Bama Theatre until later.

DIAMOND

Woolworth's Cafe
STILLMAN

It was experiences like these that made young people determined to take action and push for change. Wanting better for their children, young high school and college students began to participate in mass meetings, too. Young Black citizens began sitting at Woolworth's lunch counters across the nation to challenge unfair practices.

Although all Black citizens in Tuscaloosa city and county and the rural areas were dedicated to being treated like citizens, some were not able to participate in the march because they lived on white people's property and knew they would be punished if they participated. The saying going around was, "If you march, you move!" Even under the weight of fear and injustice, certain individuals stood out for their determination to resist.

Welcome to
Tuscaloosa

Among those shaped by this reality was Maxie Thomas, whose early life reflected both the constraints and the courage of the time. Maxie Thomas was born in a rural area in Alabama but grew up in Tuscaloosa. He had witnessed unlawful Jim Crow practices while working, and he had vowed to leave Tuscaloosa never to return. However, after realizing that racism was in Chicago as well, Maxie soon returned to Tuscaloosa.

Though he once vowed never to return, Maxie's homecoming marked the beginning of his deeper commitment to the struggle for change. He would attend mass meetings at First African Baptist church and listen to different ministers and speakers preach on plans for change. Among those ministers Maxie heard was Theophilus Yelverton Rogers, Jr., also known as T.Y. Rogers. Reverend Rogers was the minister at First African Church and was dedicated to the movement, often opening the pulpit to others to speak. Some speakers would cause the congregation to erupt in cheers.

Inspired one night by a rousing sermon, Maxie decided that he was going to protest because he wanted a better life for his children. Afraid but determined, he sat in First African Baptist church pews, ready to enter the streets of Tuscaloosa. His plan was simple yet bold: make it to the courthouse, drink from the white-only water fountain, and use the white-only restrooms. But before he and the others could step outside, chaos erupted. Molotov cocktails and smoke filled the air, and in the struggle, Maxie was struck in the face with a bat while trying to shield a young woman.

Inside the church, the scene quickly turned into panic. While tear gas filled the church, teenage children, Stillman College students, and other determined citizens were afraid. They began screaming, hiding, and trying to take cover as angry white citizens invaded the church. Someone lost their shoe in the violent scramble as they scattered all over the church. Although their goal was to march to the courthouse, some were overtaken by law enforcement and an angry mob of white citizens inside the church.

Outside, the violence only grew worse. The peaceful marchers on the outside were struck by objects and screamed at as they headed to the courthouse. Reverend T.Y. Rogers was immediately arrested and could see the siege erupt as he sat in a paddy wagon with tears. He was not the only one arrested that day.

POLICE

DRUID
DRAGONS

Many Black citizens went to jail that day, but they were still determined to fight for their rights. While in jail, some of the Black people did not receive care until they began yelling, screaming, and demanding they be seen by a doctor. Maxie, among those in jail, was seriously injured after the violent church scuffle. Thus, many of the jailed Black citizens, including Albert Ike, became uncontrollable until Maxie underwent medical treatment for his gash. Even after the arrests and injuries, the struggle continued in the battle over how the events were remembered.

Although the white citizens dismantled the peaceful protest, that day was printed as "Scattered Violence Reported" in the New York Times. Yet even with so much pain and loss, the truth of what happened could not be hidden. Black newspapers told what had truly unfolded as their own left First African Church. The misrepresentation would not stop the fight from moving forward.

The New York Times.
Scatterd Violence Reported
THE BIRMINGHAM TIMES
Telling The Truth About Bloody Tuesday

WHITE
ONLY

In the coming weeks, the Black citizens were able to march to the courthouse peacefully that summer of 1964, which was dubbed "Freedom Summer." On June 25, 1964, a federal judge ordered the removal of the segregated signs. This act was considered a win for the Black citizens who worked tirelessly for equality and justice. In the years that followed, many who had marched carried those lessons into their lives and communities.

Maxie Thomas remained in Tuscaloosa, where he raised his family and owned several record stores throughout Alabama. The foot soldiers from the local schools of Druid, Riverside, Bolter, Stillman College, and the rural areas went in multiple directions. Their feet planted them as doctors, lawyers, teachers, morticians, mechanics, engineers, writers, ministers, and a plethora of fields that they chose in Alabama and all over the world. Lastly, after Bloody Tuesday, Black men created an organization called the Defenders to protect their neighborhoods and their people. What began as marches in the streets became footsteps that echoed across the world, carrying with them the legacy of freedom and progress.

Thomas TV & Records

ECHO OF THE COMMUNITY

Gina Rogers, T Y Rogers' daughter, was the first African American student to integrate Oakdale Elementary School. Dr. George Augustus Weaver, one of the first Black physicians in Tuscaloosa, served at Stillman Hospital on the campus of Stillman College. A devoted member of First African Baptist Church, he graciously opened his private book collection to African Americans, nurturing minds and expanding opportunities during segregation. Ruth Bolden, the branch's first librarian, was not initially recognized, yet her faithful service and commitment to literacy were later honored alongside his. Together, the Weaver-Bolden name endures as a beautiful echo of community, learning, and service.

ABOUT THE AUTHOR

Marlisa Wiggins is a devoted English teacher from Tuscaloosa, Alabama, with a deep-seated passion for history. Her fascination with Tuscaloosa's local African American history ignited unexpectedly while watching a news segment about civil rights demonstrations that had occurred right in her hometown — events she had never known about. This revelation led to profound discussions with her parents and countless hours spent watching historical footage, drawing her ever deeper into the stories of her community.

www.ingramcontent.com/pod-product-compliance
Lightning Source LLC
LaVergne TN
LVHW070159110826
845147LV00002B/447
* 9 7 9 8 9 9 5 1 3 8 3 0 3 *